SCIENCE ESSENTIALS CHEMISTRY

Chemical Reactions

DENISE WALKER

Evans

EVANS

LONDON

541.3

© Evans Brothers Ltd 2007

Published by:
Evans Brothers
2a Portman Mansions
Chiltern Street
London W1U 6NR

Series editor:
Harriet Brown

Editor:
Harriet Brown

Design:
Simon Morse

Illustrations:
Ian Thompson, Simon Morse

Printed in China by
WKT Company Limited

British Library Cataloguing in
Publication Data

Walker, Denise
  Chemical reactions. - (Science
essentials. Chemistry)
  1. Chemical reactions - Juvenile
literature
  I. Title
  541.3'9

ISBN-10: 0-237-53001-5

ISBN-13: 978-0-237-53001-3

Contents

4   Introduction

6   CHAPTER 1
Physical and chemical changes

10   CHAPTER 2
How to start a chemical reaction

12   CHAPTER 3
Exothermic and endothermic reactions

14   CHAPTER 4
Understanding equations

20   CHAPTER 5
Decomposition, precipitation and combustion

24   CHAPTER 6
Displacement reactions

26   CHAPTER 7
Reversible reactions

28   CHAPTER 8
Electrolysis

32   CHAPTER 9
Analysing chemical reactions

36   CHAPTER 10
Biological reactions

38   CHAPTER 11
How to speed up a reaction

46   Glossary and answers

48   Index

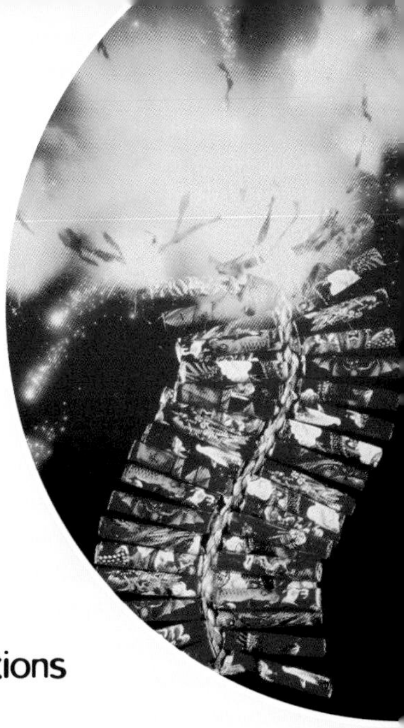

Introduction

Chemical reactions are continually taking place on our planet. They occur inside our bodies, inside plants and other animals, in the atmosphere and beneath the Earth's

surface. We have learnt a great deal about chemical reactions and have discovered how to adapt them for our own use.

This book takes you on a journey to discover more about chemical reactions. Find out how they work, what they can do and why we need them. Learn all about reactions that give out heat and find out why some reactions freeze. We take a closer look at chemical equations and show that they are not as complicated as they might appear. You can also find out the difference between physical and chemical changes, discover how to start a reaction and understand how to speed up a chemical reaction.

This book also contains feature boxes that will help you to unravel more about the mysteries of chemical reactions. Test yourself on what you have learnt so far; investigate some of the concepts discussed; find out more key facts; and discover some of the scientific findings of the past and how these might be utilised in the future.

Chemical reactions are all around us. Now you can understand how they shape our planet and allow life as we know it.

DID YOU KNOW?

▶ Watch out for these boxes – they contain surprising and fascinating facts about chemical reactions in the world around us.

TEST YOURSELF

▶ Use these boxes to see how much you've learnt. Try to answer the questions without looking at the book, but take a look if you are really stuck.

INVESTIGATE

▶ These boxes contain experiments that you can carry out at home. The equipment you will need is usually cheap and easy to find around the home.

TIME TRAVEL

▶ These boxes describe scientific discoveries from the past and fascinating developments that pave the way for the advance of science in the future.

ANSWERS

At the end of this book on pages 46 and 47, you will find the answers to the questions from the 'Test yourself' and 'Investigate' boxes.

GLOSSARY

Words highlighted in **bold** are described in detail in the glossary on pages 46 and 47.

Physical and chemical changes

Many substances change naturally over time. Rocks change gradually as a result of weathering, and water changes when the temperature rises or falls. Some substances change when other substances join them as a result of chemical reactions. Any change can be classified as either a physical or a chemical change.

PHYSICAL CHANGE

Physical change occurs when the properties of a substance change but its chemical composition does not. The properties of a substance are how it looks, feels or acts. Consider an ice cube that **melts** when it is taken out of the freezer. Ice is frozen water and as it melts, it changes into liquid water. Its physical state of matter has changed, but it is still water.

THE CHANGE FROM SOLID TO LIQUID TO GAS

Solid

Liquid

A water molecule consists of two hydrogen atoms joined together with one oxygen atom: H_2O. When ice melts, the forces holding the molecules together weaken but the molecules themselves remain unchanged. This is a physical change. If liquid water is heated, it will **boil** and turn into gaseous water, called steam. During boiling, the molecules gain energy from the heat. The weak forces between the water molecules in the liquid break and they are able to move further and further away from each other. But they are still water molecules. Again, this is a physical change.

Physical changes can be easily reversed as we see during **condensation** and **freezing**. When molecules cool down, they lose energy and become less active. This means that they do not stray as far from each other and forces can re-form between them.

◀ The particles in a solid are tightly bound together. The particles in a liquid are only loosely bound, and in a gas they are not bound at all.

Gas

Miscible and immiscible

Adding chemicals together can also result in a physical change, but only if the chemical composition does not change. When oil and water are added together there is no chemical change. Oil and water do not mix – they are **immiscible**. The forces between the water molecules are much stronger than those between the water and the oil molecules, and so the substances do not mix.

▲ Oil floats on water. The two substances do not mix.

Liquids that do mix, such as ink and water, are called **miscible** substances. The forces between the ink and the water molecules are the same and so they mix. Although they mix, they are still only undergoing a physical change. The ink molecules and the water molecules do not change their form.

Physical changes include changes in the following:

▶ State of matter
▶ Appearance
▶ Strength
▶ Hardness
▶ How well they conduct electricity
▶ Size

CHEMICAL CHANGE

A chemical change is when the chemical composition of a substance changes. This is usually caused by a chemical reaction. Chemical reactions begin with one or more substances, called **reactants**, and end with at least one completely new substance, or **product**.

Chemical reactions can be sudden, or they can take place over very long periods of time. They may be obvious, or we may not be able to notice anything at all. It is only by studying the chemicals before and afterwards that we can tell whether a change has occurred.

Chemical bonds

During a chemical change, **chemical bonds** break and form. During the formation of salt, for example, sodium atoms react with chlorine molecules. This chemical reaction forms sodium chloride, which forms the salt that we put on our food. Chemical bonds have formed between the sodium and the chlorine.

Chemical changes are more permanent than physical changes. They cannot be easily reversed because chemical bonds cannot be easily broken. An example of this is the formation of rust. The chemical name for rust is hydrated iron (III) oxide. It forms by a reaction between iron, water and oxygen. It would seem an easy solution to just scrape the rust from our bicycles to reveal the shiny, strong metal beneath. However, the metal beneath will be thin and **corroded**. Rusting cannot be easily reversed, and further rusting can only be prevented by coating the metal so that oxygen and water cannot attack it.

EXPLOSIONS

Chemical reactions can be extremely dramatic, noisy and colourful. An explosion is a chemical change that involves a high temperature, the sudden and violent release of energy and light, and the production of gases. Explosions are **combustion** (burning) reactions and require the presence of oxygen. They are often associated with death and destruction, but this is not the only side to them. They are essential to the mining industry to blast apart rocks in the search for valuable minerals from the Earth's crust. Explosions can also be used for thrust in rockets and jet engines, and are the basis of fireworks.

Traditional fireworks such as the firecrackers used for Chinese New Year contain gunpowder. Gunpowder is 75 per cent potassium nitrate, 15 per cent charcoal and 10 per cent sulphur. When these chemicals are ignited, they undergo the following chemical reactions:

▶ Charcoal burns to produce a mixture of carbon dioxide and carbon monoxide.

▶ Potassium nitrate releases oxygen.

▶ Sulphur reacts with oxygen to produce sulphur dioxide.

As the chemicals are contained within a paper case, the pressure of the gaseous products quickly builds up and the cracker 'explodes'. The result is a very loud noise and a lot of smoke.

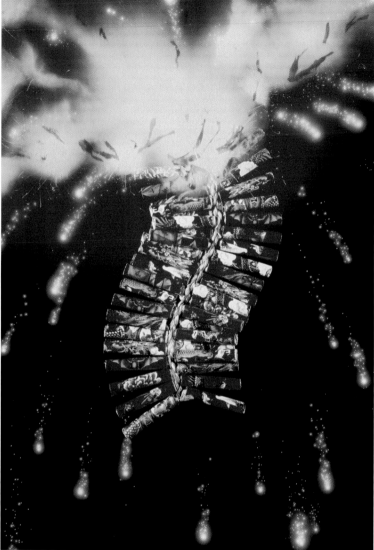

▼ This firecracker is exploding. The chemicals are contained within the cylindrical bangers. They are joined together by a fuse along which a spark travels.

DID YOU KNOW?

▶ The largest firework ever produced was called Universe I Part II. It was a five-colour firework and was exploded as part of the Lake Toya Festival in Japan in 1988. The shell weighed 700 kilogrammes, which is roughly the same weight as a cow, and was 1.4 metres in diameter. When it was exploded, it produced a display that was an incredible 1.2 kilometres in diameter.

EXPLOSIONS IN CARS

When a petrol engine is switched on, the petrol and oxygen in the air mix together and are ignited by the spark plugs. The result of this chemical reaction is a mini-explosion, which releases carbon dioxide, nitrogen oxides and steam. These gaseous products force a piston to move, which turns parts of the engine that are ultimately connected to the wheels of the car, making motion possible.

EXPLOSIONS IN ROCKETS

Rockets are also propelled using explosions, but the principle is slightly different. A turning action is not produced. Instead, the products of the explosion are directed in one way, forcing movement in the other. This is a little like leaving a hosepipe running without holding it at the end. The pressure of the water that comes out of the hosepipe forces the pipe to spin and fly around.

In rockets, a solid or liquid fuel is used. The earliest rockets were used in warfare by the Chinese in the 1200s. They were powered by gunpowder. Today, liquid fuels power the main engines of space shuttles and spacecraft such as Cassini. Cassini arrived at Saturn in 2004, and is still studying the planet Saturn's moons.

Liquid fuels include mixtures of liquid hydrogen and liquid oxygen, and kerosene and liquid oxygen. The fuel and an **oxidiser** are pumped into a chamber where they are ignited. When they burn, they react to create a high-pressure, high-speed plume of gases. The gases are accelerated until they are travelling up to 16,000 kilometres per hour. The force of the gases leaving the rocket propels it forwards.

TIME TRAVEL:
DISCOVERIES OF THE PAST

Unplanned explosions were a common occurrence in coal mines until the invention of the Davy lamp, in 1815. Coal mines are a source of methane, which is a flammable gas. In the past, coal miners used candles to light their way. Pockets of methane gas would explode dangerously when ignited by the candle's flame. The Davy lamp was safer because it contained the candle and spread the heat from the flame over a metal gauze. By doing this, the temperature of the metal gauze could not become high enough to ignite the methane. The Davy lamp could also be used to detect flammable gases. The candle would burn with a bluer flame if such gases were present.

▼ This rocket burns solid and liquid fuel to lift the shuttle into orbit 640 kilometres above the Earth's surface.

INVESTIGATE

Find out whether the following changes are physical or chemical.
(1) Stage smoke – Solid carbon dioxide turns to gaseous carbon dioxide.
(2) Hydrogen and oxygen change into water.
(3) Hand warmers.

How to start a chemical reaction

The atoms within a molecule are held together by chemical bonds. In order for reactants (the chemicals you begin with) to become products, the bonds must be broken. This requires energy. To break just a few bonds and begin a chemical reaction, energy is added in the form of heat, motion, water or light.

STARTING A REACTION

(1) HEAT

Heat energy causes the reactants' atoms to move around. As they move, the bonds between the atoms begin to break. When heat is added, the molecules also collide with one another more frequently. This also breaks the chemical bonds.

(2) MOTION

Stirring can provide enough energy to trigger the bonds to break. Some chemicals are sensitive to touch and will react with the slightest motion.

(3) WATER

Some metals are very reactive when exposed to water. Potassium is extremely reactive with water and the reaction releases a lot of heat energy. This heat accelerates the reaction even further. In fact, the explosive reaction of potassium with water is just an extremely fast and violent version of rusting!

(4) LIGHT

Light energy can break chemical bonds and start a reaction. Non-digital camera film is a paper soaked in light-sensitive silver chloride. When a photo is taken, light enters the camera and darkens the silver chloride. This leaves an image called a negative. The negative can be converted into a photograph.

Light initiates the most important chemical reaction on our planet – photosynthesis. This is a reaction in plants between carbon dioxide and water.

◄ The reaction between potassium metal and water produces enough heat to melt the potassium.

WHAT HAPPENS DURING A CHEMICAL REACTION?

The input of energy frees some atoms from their compounds. They look for new atoms with which to combine. The freed atoms attack the other reactants and force them to give up their chemical bonds. Very soon, all of the freed atoms rearrange themselves into new combinations that we call products.

ENERGY

During a chemical reaction, energy changes its form. Initially, chemical energy is stored in the chemical bonds. The reaction begins once heat energy, light energy or motion energy break some of the bonds. This releases the chemical energy. Energy is produced in the form of sound and light, and heat energy can be lost or gained. At the end of the reaction, energy is again contained within chemical bonds.

There is usually less energy within the chemical bonds of the products than there is in the chemical bonds of the reactants. Most reactions would not take place if this was not the case. For example, a ball will roll down a hill because it has more energy at the top of the hill than at the bottom. It will not spontaneously roll up a hill for precisely the same reason. The same is true for chemical reactions.

TEST YOURSELF

▶ How are each of the following reactions started?

(1) A mixture of chlorine and hydrogen react together to give hydrogen chloride when exposed to a photographic flash.

(2) Iron and oxygen will react together to form rust. This is a very slow reaction.

When dealing with chemical reactions, it is important to know the following terms:

Type of particle	Definition
Atom	Simplest form of a substance
Molecule	Two or more atoms chemically bonded together
Ion	An atom with a positive or negative charge or a small group of charged atoms
Element	A substance made from one type of atom that cannot be broken down chemically
Compound	Two or more elements chemically bonded together

TIME TRAVEL: DISCOVERIES OF THE PAST

In 1826, John Walker, a British chemist, noticed that motion could cause a chemical reaction. He stirred potassium carbonate and antimony (a metal) together and then scraped the stick on the floor to remove a blob of mixture. To his surprise, the stick caught fire. This began the invention of matches. Antimony was replaced with phosphorus. Unfortunately, the first matches were dangerous because the phosphorus poisoned the matchmakers. The matchmakers clothes also caught fire because of the sensitive nature of the chemical mixture. Safety matches (see right) were invented in 1844. The match carries the reactant – potassium chlorate – and the strip on the box contains phosphorus. The match catches fire when it is struck on the strip.

Exothermic and endothermic reactions

During a chemical reaction, energy changes from one type to another. The chemical bonds break and re-form. We cannot see these changes happen but we can observe clues such as colour changes, sounds and smells. One of the most common changes is a change in temperature. If we place a very sensitive thermometer in a chemical reaction, we can see that it has either warmed – an **exothermic** reaction – or cooled – an **endothermic** reaction. Thermodynamics is the study of the conversions between heat and other forms of energy.

EXOTHERMIC REACTIONS

Reactions that give out heat energy are called exothermic reactions. These reactions feel warm to the touch. If a reaction is highly exothermic, it may be dangerous to touch. Explosions are very exothermic reactions. We use a thermometer or temperature probe to detect temperature changes.

Energy is required to break chemical bonds, which means that energy is spent, or used up. As the atoms rearrange themselves and form new chemical bonds, energy is released, often in the form of heat. In an exothermic reaction, the total energy released in the formation of new bonds is greater than the total energy used to break the bonds. Therefore, overall the reaction will heat up.

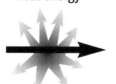

Heat energy

Reactants   Products

Exothermic reactions are very common because the products have less energy stored in the chemical bonds than the reactants. This is an ideal situation because one of the 'laws of thermodynamics' predicts that all reactants and products will try to contain as little energy as possible.

Combustion reactions are exothermic (see pages 22-23). When methane burns in oxygen, it produces carbon dioxide and water.

Methane
+
Oxygen

Carbon dioxide
+
Water

Methane contains more energy than carbon dioxide and water. This extra energy is released as heat when methane breaks down.

▲ Landfill sites give off methane gas. This can build up and explode in a violent exothermic reaction. To prevent this, it is gradually burnt off instead.

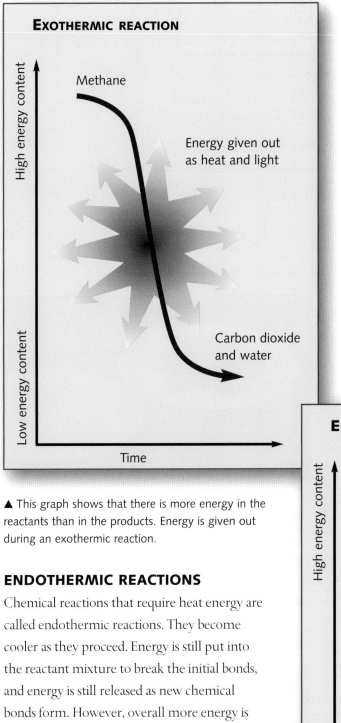

EXOTHERMIC REACTION

Methane

Energy given out as heat and light

Carbon dioxide and water

High energy content

Low energy content

Time

▲ This graph shows that there is more energy in the reactants than in the products. Energy is given out during an exothermic reaction.

ENDOTHERMIC REACTIONS

Chemical reactions that require heat energy are called endothermic reactions. They become cooler as they proceed. Energy is still put into the reactant mixture to break the initial bonds, and energy is still released as new chemical bonds form. However, overall more energy is absorbed by the reaction than is released. The products of endothermic reactions contain more energy than the reactants.

When barium hydroxide is mixed with ammonium chloride, the reaction is so endothermic that it can freeze water.

Heat energy

Reactants ➡ Products

Another endothermic reaction occurs when you suck on a sherbet sweet. The sherbet (citric acid and sodium hydrogencarbonate) and the water in your mouth react together. The reaction takes in heat from your mouth, which makes it feel cold.

▼ This graph shows that there is less energy in the reactants than in the products. Energy is taken in during an endothermic reaction.

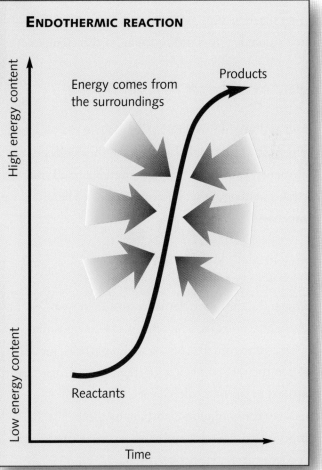

ENDOTHERMIC REACTION

Energy comes from the surroundings

Products

High energy content

Low energy content

Reactants

Time

Understanding equations

Although many adjectives are used to describe chemical reactions, words are not the most efficient way of explaining them. Chemists working around the world need to share their ideas, and it is easier if they speak the same 'language'. In the case of chemistry, this language is chemical formulae and chemical equations.

WORD EQUATIONS

In a word equation, the names of the reactants are written on the left hand side and the names of the products on the right hand side. The two sides are separated by the symbol ⟶ which means 'goes to'. Therefore, in a chemical reaction, the reactants 'go to' the products.

IRON AND SULPHUR

Iron and sulphur are both elements. When they react together they produce a compound called iron sulphide. The word equation for this change is:

Iron + Sulphur ⟶ Iron sulphide

▲ Iron (left) and sulphur (right).

Iron and sulphur will only react to form iron sulphide if heat is added. The heat is responsible for breaking the bonds present within each of the elements. The atoms that have been liberated react with each other. Heat is neither a reactant nor a product. Therefore, we write the equation like this:

$$\text{Iron} + \text{Sulphur} \xrightarrow{\text{heat}} \text{Iron sulphide}$$

▼ Iron sulphide is a hard and non-magnetic compound.

Iron and sulphur are elements with their own distinctive properties. Sulphur is a yellow powder with a strong smell. Iron is a shiny magnetic metal. When they are combined together, these properties are lost in the iron sulphide. If a magnet is held close to the compound, nothing happens. The product has different properties to the reactants. A chemical change has occurred.

HYDROGEN AND CHLORINE

Hydrogen and chlorine gas react together slowly, but when they are exposed to ultraviolet light, the reaction can become violent. This reaction can be represented as follows:

$$\text{Hydrogen + Chlorine} \xrightarrow{\text{u.v.}} \text{Hydrogen chloride}$$

HYDROGEN PEROXIDE

Hydrogen peroxide is a colourless liquid that decomposes to produce water and oxygen. The process is very slow, but can be speeded up by using a compound called manganese dioxide. This chemical is a **catalyst**. A catalyst is a substance that alters a chemical reaction (usually by speeding it up) without being changed itself. Manganese dioxide is not used up and so it is neither a reactant nor a product. In fact, at the end of the reaction, the black powder of manganese dioxide can still be seen in the bottom of the test tube. The word equation for this change is:

$$\text{Hydrogen peroxide} \xrightarrow{\text{Manganese dioxide}} \text{Water + Oxygen}$$

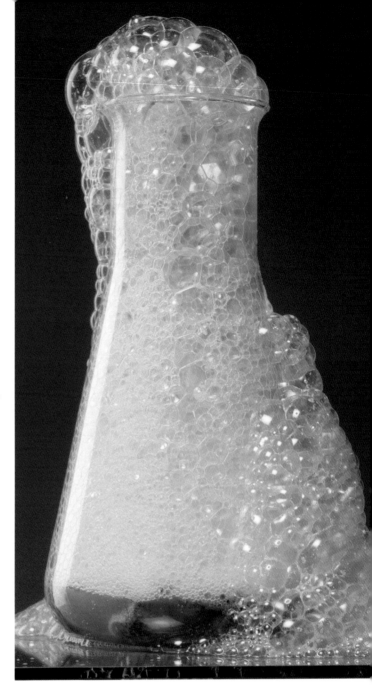

▶ This flask contains hydrogen peroxide and some raw liver. Liver contains an **enzyme** (a biological catalyst) called catalase. It causes the breakdown of hydrogen peroxide to accelerate in a similar way to manganese dioxide. You can see the bubbles of oxygen that have formed.

TEST YOURSELF

▶ Write word equations to represent the following chemical changes.
Try to include as much detail as you can.

(1) Carbon reacts with oxygen in the presence of heat to form carbon dioxide.
(2) Magnesium burns in oxygen to form magnesium oxide.
(3) Methane and chlorine react in the presence of ultraviolet light to form chloromethane and hydrogen chloride.
(4) Hydrogen peroxide decomposes to water and oxygen in the presence of the catalyst catalase.

CHEMICAL FORMULAE

Word equations are a good but simple way of representing a chemical change. However, word equations have their limits. They do not tell us exactly how the atoms rearrange themselves. For a fuller understanding of a chemical change we must write a chemical equation. Chemical equations contain chemical formulae, rather than words.

ELEMENTS IN CHEMICAL REACTIONS

If elements are present as either reactants or products, it is quicker to use their chemical symbols. You can find the chemical symbols in the Periodic Table and in the list of elements on this page.

Some elements go around as pairs of atoms. When they are present in a chemical equation, we write them with a small '2' following their symbol, as shown in the table above right.

Element	Written in an equation as:
Chlorine	Cl_2
Oxygen	O_2
Nitrogen	N_2
Hydrogen	H_2
Bromine	Br_2
Fluorine	F_2
Iodine	I_2

ELEMENTS AND THEIR SYMBOLS

You can use this list to find out the names of the more common elements.

Ac = Actinium
Ag = Silver
Al = Aluminium
Ar = Argon
As = Arsenic
At = Astatine
Au = Gold
B = Boron
Ba = Barium
Be = Beryllium
Br = Bromine
C = Carbon
Ca = Calcium
Cd = Cadmium
Cl = Chlorine
Co = Cobalt
Cr = Chromium
Cs = Caesium
Cu = Copper
F = Fluorine
Fe = Iron

Ga = Gallium
Ge = Germanium
H = Hydrogen
He = Helium
Hf = Hafnium
Hg = Mercury
I = Iodine
Ir = Iridium
K = Potassium
Kr = Krypton
Li = Lithium
Mg = Magnesium
Mn = Manganese
Mo = Molybdenum
N = Nitrogen
Na = Sodium
Nb = Niobium
Ne = Neon
Ni = Nickel
O = Oxygen
P = Phosporous

Pb = Lead
Pd = Palladium
Pt = Platinum
Ra = Radium
Rb = Rubidium
Rh = Rhodium
Rn = Radon
S = Sulphur
Sb = Antimony
Sc = Scandium
Se = Selenium
Si = Silicon
Sn = Tin
Sr = Strontium
Ta = Tantalum
Ti = Titanium
V = Vanadium
W = Tungsten
Xe = Xenon
Zn = Zinc
Zr = Zirconium

THE PERIODIC TABLE

1 H		Metals															

Metals
Non-metals

1 2 —— Groups

Atomic number

1 H																	2 He
3 Li	4 Be											5 B	6 C	7 N	8 O	9 F	10 Ne
11 Na	12 Mg											13 Al	14 Si	15 P	16 S	17 Cl	18 Ar
19 K	20 Ca	21 Sc	22 Ti	23 V	24 Cr	25 Mn	26 Fe	27 Co	28 Ni	29 Cu	30 Zn	31 Ga	32 Ge	33 As	34 Se	35 Br	36 Kr
37 Rb	38 Sr	39 Y	40 Zr	41 Nb	42 Mo	43 Tc	44 Ru	45 Rh	46 Pd	47 Ag	48 Cd	49 In	50 Sn	51 Sb	52 Te	53 I	54 Xe
55 Cs	56 Ba	57 La	72 Hf	73 Ta	74 W	75 Re	76 Os	77 Ir	78 Pt	79 Au	80 Hg	81 Tl	82 Pb	83 Bi	84 Po	85 At	86 Rn
87 Fr	88 Ra	89 Ac	104 Rf	105 Db	106 Sg	107 Bh	108 Hs	109 Mt	110 Ds	111 Rg							

58 Ce	59 Pr	60 Nd	61 Pm	62 Sm	63 Eu	64 Gd	65 Tb	66 Dy	67 Ho	68 Er	69 Tm	70 Yb	71 Lu
90 Th	91 Pa	92 U	93 Np	94 Pu	95 Am	96 Cm	97 Bk	98 Cf	99 Es	100 Fm	101 Md	102 No	103 Lr

COMPOUNDS IN CHEMICAL EQUATIONS

You will gradually learn the chemical formulae of compounds as you see them written down time and time again. However, you can work out some of the simple compounds using a method called 'swap and drop'.

The components of a certain type of compound are called ions. Ions form when atoms gain or lose negatively-charged electrons during chemical reactions. Sodium atoms each lose an electron to become sodium ions. Sodium atoms have the symbol Na. Therefore, sodium ions have the symbol Na^+. By losing one electron, the sodium gains a positive charge because it now has one more proton than electrons. Remember, protons have a positive charge and electrons have a negative charge.

Sodium atoms will always lose only one electron. This is because they have one electron in the outer shell of their atoms. The next shell in has a complete set of eight electrons. If the sodium can lose its outermost electron, the next shell in becomes the outer shell. Atoms with a full outer shell of electrons are much more stable than those with partially-filled shells.

SWAP AND DROP:
SODIUM + CHLORINE

When sodium and chlorine react together, each sodium atom loses an electron to a chlorine atom. This forms sodium ions, Na^+, and chloride ions, Cl^-. We can determine the formula of the compound using the following steps:

(1) Write the number on the charge beneath the ion. The symbols $^+$ and $^-$ on their own refer to $^{1+}$ and $^{1-}$.

(2) Swap the numbers around and 'drop' them to the ground.

(3) This tells us that we need one sodium ion to balance out one chloride ion. The formula is therefore NaCl.

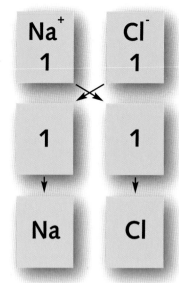

MAGNESIUM + CHLORINE

To gain a full outer shell of electrons magnesium loses its outer two electrons. As an ion it has two more protons than electrons. Its formula is Mg^{2+}.

By carrying out swap and drop, we find out that we need one Mg ion to balance two Cl ions. The formula is $MgCl_2$.

Here are the symbols and charges for some common ions:

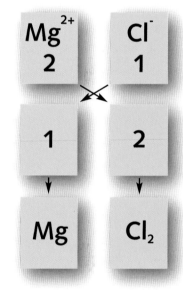

3+	2+	1+	1-	2-
Aluminium Al^{3+}	Magnesium Mg^{2+}	Sodium Na^+	Chloride Cl^-	Oxide O^{2-}
Iron(III) Fe^{3+}	Iron Fe^{2+}	Lithium Li^+	Bromide Br^-	Sulphide S^{2-}
Manganese(III) Mn^{3+}	Copper Cu^{2+}	Potassium K^+	Hydroxide OH^-	Carbonate CO_3^{2-}
Chromium(III) Cr^{3+}	Calcium Ca^{2+}	Hydrogen H^+	Nitrate NO_3^-	Sulphate SO_4^{2-}

The formulae for the compounds in the table below cannot easily be determined. Use this table as a reference:

Name	Formula
Water	H_2O
Carbon dioxide	CO_2
Hydrochloric acid	HCl
Sulphuric acid	H_2SO_4
Sodium hydroxide	$NaOH$

TEST YOURSELF

▶ Use the 'swap and drop' method to work out the formulae of the following compounds.

(1) Copper oxide

(2) Iron chloride

(3) Aluminium bromide

(4) Calcium oxide

BALANCING CHEMICAL EQUATIONS

During every chemical reaction, reactants turn into products. We do not lose or gain any atoms during a chemical reaction. Every atom must be found on both sides of the equation. Therefore, we must make sure all chemical equations are balanced. For example, consider the following chemical change, which is a common burning reaction.

Carbon + Oxygen $\longrightarrow$ Carbon dioxide
$C + O_2 \longrightarrow CO_2$

One atom of carbon combines with two atoms of oxygen to give one molecule of carbon dioxide.

On each side of the equation there is one carbon atom and two oxygen atoms. The equation is balanced.

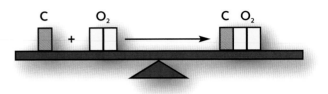

Once you are confident that you can carry through the 'swap and drop' method from the previous page, and that you have learnt the common formulae, then work through the following stages to practise balancing equations.

(1) Write a word equation.

Potassium + Water $\longrightarrow$ Potassium hydroxide + Hydrogen

(2) Convert the word equation into symbols.

$K + H_2O \longrightarrow KOH + H_2$

(3) Count the number of each type of atom on either side of the arrow in the equation. Where there is a small '2' next to the H, it means that there are two atoms of hydrogen. In this example we have:

On the left hand side: On the right hand side:

1 x K	1 x K
1 x O	1 x O
2 x H	3 x H

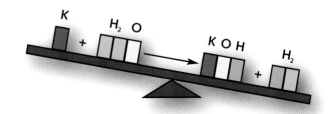

If the numbers on each side are the same, no further adjustments are necessary. If not, we must balance the equation by using large numbers at the front of a formula. The large number means that all atoms in the formula are multiplied by it. In our example, the number of hydrogen atoms is unbalanced. This can be amended by inserting the following numbers.

$$2K + 2H_2O \longrightarrow 2KOH + H_2$$

We now have the following:

On the left hand side:	On the right hand side:
2 x K	2 x K
2 x O	2 x O
4 x H	4 x H

The number of atoms on each side is the same and so our equation is balanced.

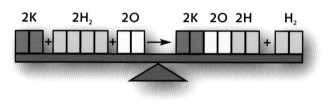

2K   2H₂   2O   2K 2O 2H   H₂

STATE SYMBOLS

These are symbols that show the physical state of each of the reactants and products and can be seen in the table below.

State symbol	What does it mean?
(s)	Solid
(l)	Liquid
(g)	Gas
(aq)	Aqueous; dissolved in water

When we add the state symbols, our example now becomes:

$$2K_{(s)} + 2H_2O_{(l)} \longrightarrow 2KOH_{(aq)} + H_{2(g)}$$

To find out the natural state of the reactants and products, you will need to look them up in a reference book or on the internet.

The final equation tells us that:
(1) Two atoms of potassium react with two molecules of water.
(2) The products are two molecules of potassium hydroxide and one molecule of hydrogen.
(3) The potassium is solid. The water is liquid and the potassium hydroxide is aqueous. We may see bubbles of hydrogen gas.

TEST YOURSELF

▶ Write balanced chemical equations for each of the following reactions:

(1) Hydrogen reacts with oxygen to form water.

(2) Sodium reacts with chlorine to form sodium chloride.

(3) Magnesium reacts with oxygen to form magnesium oxide.

▼ **This magnesium ribbon is burning in air, which contains oxygen, to form magnesium oxide.**

Decomposition, precipitation and combustion

Millions of different chemical reactions occur every day. Reactions in our bodies keep us alive and well, while reactions in our vehicles make them move. Chemists classify reactions according to how they work. Three common types of chemical reaction are thermal decomposition, precipitation and combustion.

▲ These chalk cliffs are mainly made from calcium carbonate, or limestone.

THERMAL DECOMPOSITION

Decomposition is when a single substance breaks down into two or more products. If this change occurs under the influence of heat, then it is called thermal decomposition. Decomposition reactions can also be caused by light.

Calcium carbonate (limestone) undergoes thermal decomposition when it is heated. This reaction produces calcium oxide and carbon dioxide. Calcium oxide is also known as lime. Lime is used in agriculture to neutralise acidic soil.

HYDRATED COMPOUNDS

Hydrated compounds undergo thermal decomposition. They have water molecules in their structures. When hydrated copper sulphate is heated, the water is driven out. It has the formula $CuSO_4.5H_2O$ and is a crystal. When it is heated, the water **evaporates** and leaves behind anhydrous (without water) copper sulphate. This thermal decomposition is characterised by a colour change from blue to grey/white.

◀ Hydrated copper sulphate is blue.

▼ Anhydrous copper sulphate is grey/white.

Anhydrous copper sulphate is used to create dry environments by absorbing water from the atmosphere. It is similar to the packets of silica gel that we find in a new pair of shoes. Silica gel keeps the shoes dry and prevents the leather from becoming damaged.

One of the first anaesthetics was produced through thermal decomposition. In 1772, a British chemist, Joseph Priestley, discovered nitrous oxide. Nitrous oxide is one of the products of the thermal decomposition of a fertiliser called ammonium nitrate. Then, in the 1790s, Sir Humphry Davy investigated the effects that this gas had on people. He tested it on both himself and on his friends, and found that it dulled the sensation of pain. It became more commonly known as 'laughing gas' because of its side-effects. In the 1840s, nitrous oxide first became used as an anaesthetic in dentistry and surgery.

▶ **Sir Humphry Davy developed the first ever chemical anaesthetic.**

PRECIPITATION REACTIONS

When two solutions are mixed together, they can react to form an insoluble product called a **precipitate**. It can appear as a fine powder or a dense gel-like mass. If the precipitate is fine and floating in the liquid, it is called a **suspension**.

Precipitation reactions can be used to identify components of unknown compounds. For example, precipitation can be used to test for the presence of metals. When sodium hydroxide solution is added to certain metal compounds, a distinctive coloured precipitate is observed:

◀ This image shows a dense gel-like precipitate of iron (III) hydroxide.

TEST YOURSELF

▶ A clumsy chemist put three metal compounds away one evening, but left the bottles in a damp place so that all of the labels came off. He knew that the compounds all contained metals and that one was a chloride, one a bromide and one an iodide. Design some simple chemical tests that the chemist could carry out to identify the contents of each of the three bottles. Hint: use the information in the tables on pages 21 and 34 to help you.

INVESTIGATE

▶ Chemicals called nitrates thermally decompose to produce oxygen gas and other products. This reaction is used is fireworks.

Use the library or the internet to find out how potassium nitrate causes a firework to explode.

Metal	Colour of precipitate	Name of precipitate
Copper	Blue	Copper hydroxide
Aluminium	White	Aluminium hydroxide
Iron	Rusty brown	Iron (III) hydroxide
Iron	Green	Iron (II) hydroxide

COMBUSTION REACTIONS

A combustion reaction results in a chemical change. It usually involves a reaction between a substance and oxygen in the air and gives out heat, light and other chemical products. Combustion reactions are very important to us. We combust (burn) fuels to power our vehicles.

INGREDIENTS OF A COMBUSTION REACTION

All combustion reactions require three things: oxygen, fuel and heat. These are represented in the 'fire triangle'. If any one of these ingredients is removed, then the fire will go out. This forms the basis for extinguishing a fire.

FIRE TRIANGLE

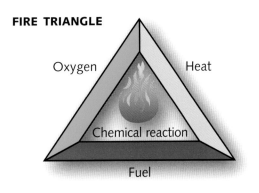

(1) HEAT

Many combustion reactions require an ignition source. Camping fuels and cookers can be lit with matches or an electronic ignition system. To start a fire, the heat must be sufficient to break the initial chemical bonds and allow the atoms to begin rearranging themselves. Overall, as the atoms reform into products, more energy is given out than was initially put in. All combustion reactions are exothermic.

(2) FUEL

When the fuel ignites, it reacts with oxygen. Once the fuel is exhausted, a fire will go out. In forest fires, there is a large supply of fuel in the form of trees. Forest fires can go on for weeks at a time causing much destruction. Every year in the USA, 17,400 square kilometres of land is burnt in forest fires. This is the equivalent of 0.18 per cent of the USA or nearly 2.5 million football pitches.

▼ Forest fires are powerful exothermic reactions. They produce intense heat and lots of smoke.

(3) OXYGEN

Air contains the oxygen necessary for a fire. Around 20 per cent of the air is oxygen gas. Some flammable chemicals are stored in an atmosphere that contains no oxygen to ensure the chemicals do not ignite. Some metals, such as sodium and potassium, are so reactive with oxygen that they are stored in oil. Water contains oxygen and so to store them in this medium would be enough to ignite the metals.

If there is sufficient oxygen, complete combustion occurs. This means that the maximum amount of chemical product is produced. When there is an insufficient amount of oxygen present, incomplete combustion occurs. This happens in the exhausts of old or poorly functioning cars.

Petrol contains the element carbon. When carbon is burnt in plenty of oxygen, it produces carbon dioxide gas. However, if it undergoes incomplete combustion, it will also give off carbon monoxide gas and small amounts of black carbon deposits called **particulates**. Although fatal if breathed in high doses, the carbon monoxide from car exhausts goes straight into the atmosphere where it disperses quickly by **diffusion**.

PUTTING OUT A FIRE

Some combustion reactions can rage out of control. To manage a fire, you must apply the basic rule of the fire triangle (see page 22). Remove one side of the triangle to put out the fire. How effective this is depends on how long the fire has been burning and how much fuel is present.

▶ Incomplete combustion is occurring in this bus. The exhaust fumes contain carbon monoxide gas and black carbon particulates.

It is important to know how fires can be safely extinguished. Fires that involve burning oil or petrol must be extinguished with sand, soil or carbon dioxide. This deprives the fire of oxygen and it quickly goes out. If water is used then the fuel will float on the water and cause the fire to spread further.

Fires caused by sparks from electrical appliances should not be extinguished using water or foam. Both of these substances conduct electricity and could cause a nasty electrical shock. Carbon dioxide and dry chemical extinguishers can be used to put out electrical fires. The electricity supply should be cut off before a fire is tackled.

Displacement reactions

In **displacement** reactions, the chemicals swap their chemical partners. For example, in the following reaction, potassium bromide reacts with chlorine. This produces potassium chloride (a compound) and bromine (an element).

Potassium bromide + Chlorine ⟶ Potassium chloride + Bromine

The chlorine has displaced (knocked out) the bromine from its compound and taken the potassium for itself.

OXIDATION AND REDUCTION

Displacement reactions are always made up of two parts; one is an oxidation reaction and the other is a reduction reaction. In the example above, the chlorine has been reduced and the bromine has been oxidised. When chemical reactants reorganise themselves into products, the new bonds form as a result of the transfer of electrons between atoms. This rearrangement of electrons is called bonding. Electrons cannot be lost from one atom unless there is another nearby to accept them.

Oxidation most commonly involves the loss of an electron and reduction involves the gain of an electron. Reduction and oxidation always occur together. This is sometimes simplified to **redox**. All displacement reactions involve an oxidation component and a reduction component and are called redox reactions.

▶ This is an iron ore quarry. Redox reactions are used to extract iron from its ore. The ore is put in a blast furnace and the following reaction takes place:

Iron oxide + Carbon monoxide ⟶ Iron + Carbon dioxide

UNDERSTANDING OXIDATION AND REDUCTION

OXIDATION – These reactions occur when any of the following happens:

▶ Electrons are lost
▶ Oxygen is gained
▶ Hydrogen is lost

Only one of these criteria needs to be met.

REDUCTION – These reactions occur when any of the following happens:

▶ Electrons are gained
▶ Oxygen is lost
▶ Hydrogen is gained

The movement of electrons is easily remembered using **OIL RIG**. This is an acronym for **O**xidation **I**s **L**oss of electrons and **R**eduction **I**s **G**ain of electrons.

Our example of a displacement (in the introduction at the top of page 24) involves the oxidation of bromine. As the reaction proceeds, the bromide part of the compound is swapped out of the compound and loses some electrons. These electrons have been transferred to the chlorine atom. So the chlorine atom has been reduced.

Obviously it is not possible to see the movement of electrons, but the chemical rules that govern how an element or compound behave state that electrons are transferred or in some cases shared.

USES FOR DISPLACEMENT REACTIONS

Chlorine is a useful substance for chemists because it is very good at taking electrons from other substances. This is the principle used for whitening paper. Chlorine is so good at taking electrons from other substances that it can actually change their colour. The colours of substances are determined by the number and position of electrons. If some electrons have been removed, the colour can change. The same principle also applies if you spill some bleach on your clothes.

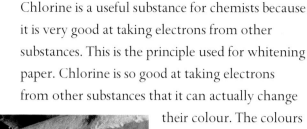

◀ This wood pulp has been bleached with chlorine. It will be poured into flat sheets and dried to make paper.

TEST YOURSELF

▶ For each of the following reactions, state which substance has been reduced and which has been oxidised. Give reasons for your choices.

(1) $CuO + H_2 \longrightarrow Cu + H_2O$

(2) $2Mg + O_2 \longrightarrow 2MgO$

(3) $2Mg + SO_2 \longrightarrow 2MgO + S$

INVESTIGATE

▶ Use the library or the internet to find out about the displacement reactions of a group of elements called the halogens. How does reactivity vary in this group and how does this result in displacement reactions?

Reversible reactions

Some reactions are described as reversible because they can proceed in both forward and reverse directions. The production of ammonia involves a reversible reaction. Ammonia is an extremely important chemical that is used as a refrigerant, a fertiliser, in water purification, in cleaning products and in explosives.

A SIMPLE REVERSIBLE REACTION

Blue copper sulphate crystals can be heated using a Bunsen burner to produce grey/white crystals of anhydrous copper sulphate. The chemical equation for this change is given below.

$$CuSO_4.5H_2O_{(s)} \xrightarrow{\text{heat}} CuSO_{4(s)} + 5H_2O_{(g)}$$

Blue copper sulphate crystals contain water molecules. When the crystals are heated the water is driven off as steam which leaves behind anhydrous copper sulphate. This reaction can be reversed by adding water to the white crystals. The crystals will appear blue once more and the

▼ This anhydrous copper sulphate is being hydrated by the addition of water. If the hydrated copper sulphate is heated, this reaction will be reversed.

chemical change that has occurred is:

$$CuSO_{4(s)} + 5H_2O_{(l)} \longrightarrow CuSO_4.5H_2O_{(s)}$$

EQUILIBRIUM

Some reversible reactions proceed in two directions at the same time. Reactions that go forwards and backwards at the same time are said to be in equilibrium. Such reactions are only possible if the products and reactants are not allowed to escape. They must be in close proximity to each other to let further reactions take place.

AMMONIA PRODUCTION

Nitrogen and hydrogen gases react together to form a gas called ammonia (NH_3).

$$N_{2(g)} + 3H_{2(g)} \longrightarrow 2NH_{3(g)}$$

As soon as the ammonia is formed, it begins to decompose back to nitrogen and hydrogen gases.

$$2NH_{3(g)} \longrightarrow N_{2(g)} + 3H_{2(g)}$$

As the two reactions occur at exactly the same time, we can use the symbol $\rightleftharpoons$. This symbol indicates that the reaction is spontaneously reversible. We can rewrite the chemical equation as:

$$N_{2(g)} + 3H_{2(g)} \rightleftharpoons 2NH_{3(g)}$$

THE PROBLEM WITH REVERSIBLE REACTIONS

In non-reversible reactions, we combine two or more reactants together and the reaction will end when all of the reactants are converted into products. However long this takes, once it is complete, it remains complete. We expect a full conversion of reactants to products.

In a reversible reaction, there is no clear end, and 100 per cent conversion is never achieved at any one time. When chemists try to produce industrial chemicals, they need to obtain as much product as possible before it is converted back to reactants. When we make ammonia in the laboratory, only small amounts of gases are involved and so the cost is minimal.

When the reaction is carried out on a larger scale as it is in industry in the Haber Process, it can be very wasteful if 100 per cent of the reactants are not converted into ammonia. In fact, the best that producers of ammonia can achieve is approximately 15 per cent at any one time. Industrial chemists have improved the reaction of nitrogen and hydrogen to make ammonia by carrying out the following steps:

▶ Carry out the reaction at a temperature of approximately 450°C.
▶ Carry out the reaction under pressure.
▶ Carry out the reaction in the presence of a catalyst.
▶ Pump unreacted gases through the reactor so that they are not wasted.

THE HABER PROCESS

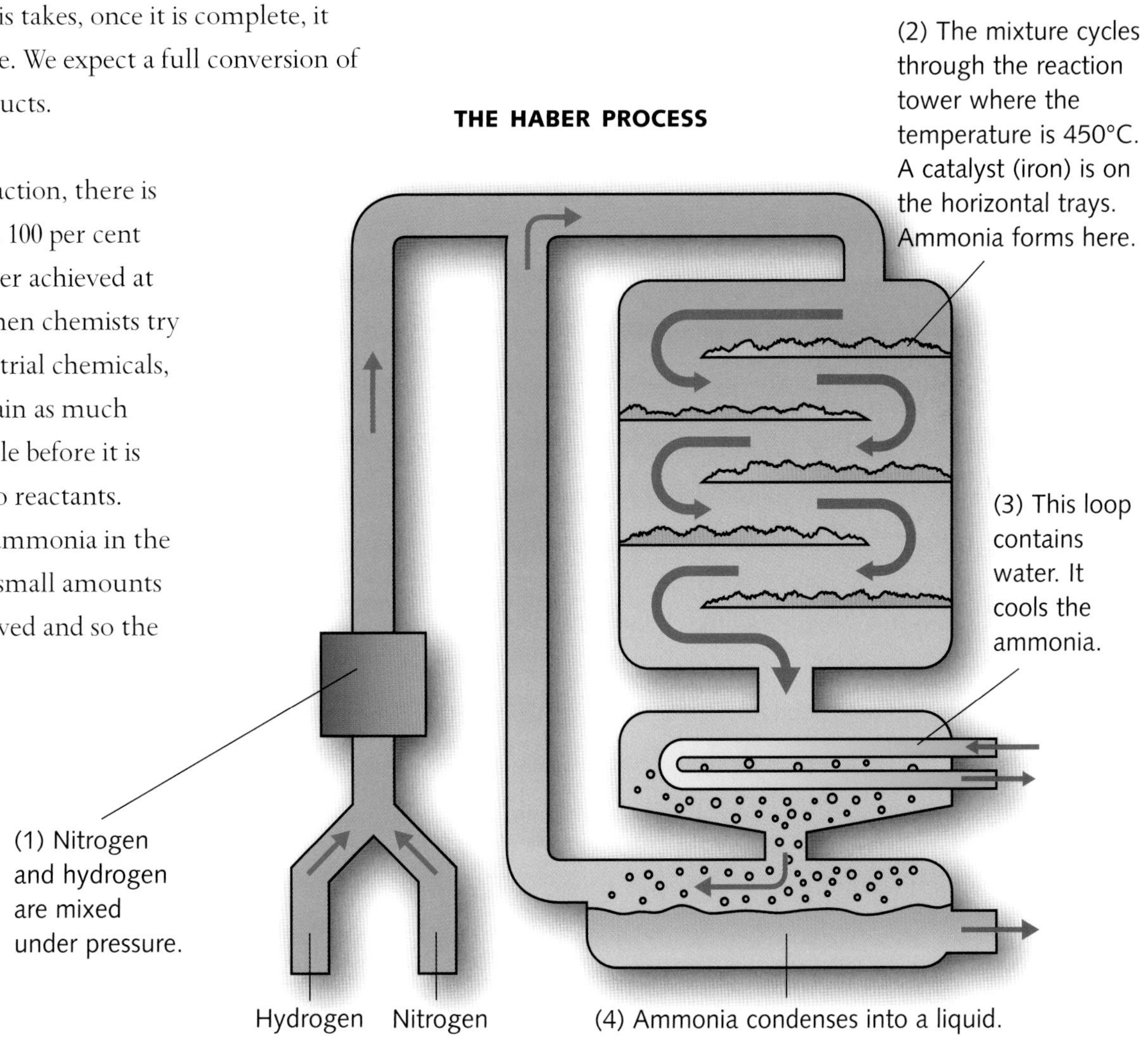

(2) The mixture cycles through the reaction tower where the temperature is 450°C. A catalyst (iron) is on the horizontal trays. Ammonia forms here.

(3) This loop contains water. It cools the ammonia.

(1) Nitrogen and hydrogen are mixed under pressure.

Hydrogen   Nitrogen

(4) Ammonia condenses into a liquid.

Electrolysis

Electrolysis is a process that uses electricity to separate bonded elements from their compounds. Before a substance can be electrolysed, it must either be melted or dissolved in a liquid that will conduct electricity. Electrolysis is used in the manufacture of sodium, aspirin, hydrogen and chlorine. It is also used in submarines to produce oxygen from seawater so that the crew can breathe.

ELECTROLYSIS OF MOLTEN COMPOUNDS

Electricity is the movement of electrons. Electrons are found in the atoms of all substances. Some of a metal's electrons are free to move around the whole substance. As they do so, they carry their negative electric charge with them. Because these electrons are not attached to any particular atom, they are said to be **delocalised**. Solids such as salt do not have free electrons and so cannot conduct electricity in this physical state.

SALT (SODIUM CHLORIDE)

When sodium and chlorine combine chemically, each sodium atom transfers an electron to a chlorine atom. Each sodium atom now has one less electron, and each chlorine atom has one more electron. The overall result is that the sodium ions have a positive charge and the chlorine ions have a negative charge. The oppositely-charged ions attract each other and form a strong chemical compound called sodium chloride.

WHAT HAPPENS TO SALT WHEN IT MELTS?

When a solid melts, its structure becomes less ordered. When salt melts, the ions are free to move away from each other and carry electrical charge. The molten salt will eventually break down into sodium and chlorine atoms. This can also happen when electricity is passed through the salt. The breakdown of a substance using electricity is called electrolysis.

STRUCTURE OF SOLID SODIUM CHLORIDE

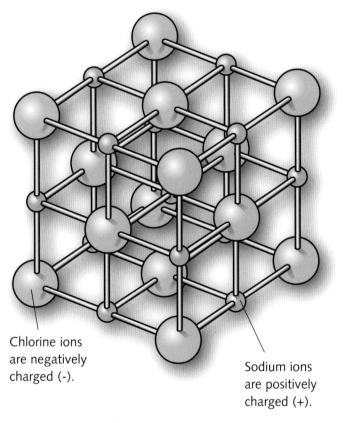

Chlorine ions are negatively charged (-).

Sodium ions are positively charged (+).

▲ Solid sodium chloride forms a large ionic lattice arrangement. The lines represent strong bonds between the atoms.

MOLTEN LEAD BROMIDE

Lead bromide is electrolysed to obtain pure lead and pure bromine. When lead bromide is melted, the lead and bromide ions break apart and are free to move. The molten lead bromide is called the electrolyte because it is the chemical that conducts electricity.

WHAT HAPPENS WHEN THE ELECTRICITY IS SWITCHED ON?

The atoms in the lead bromide break down into positively-charged lead ions and negatively-charged bromide ions. Positive ions are called **cations**. Negative ions are called **anions**. The cations (lead ions) are attracted to the electrode that is connected to the negative terminal of the electricity supply, the **cathode**. The anions (bromide ions) are attracted to the positive electrode, the **anode**.

The lead and bromide are now separated from each other. Bromide ions lose their electrons and form bromine fumes at the anode. The electrons that have been released go to the cathode. Here they combine with the lead ions to form lead metal. The lead is in liquid form because the temperature is high.

The overall reaction is:

Lead bromide $\longrightarrow$ Lead + Bromine

$PbBr_{2(l)} \longrightarrow Pb_{(l)} + Br_{2(g)}$

ELECTROLYSIS CIRCUIT

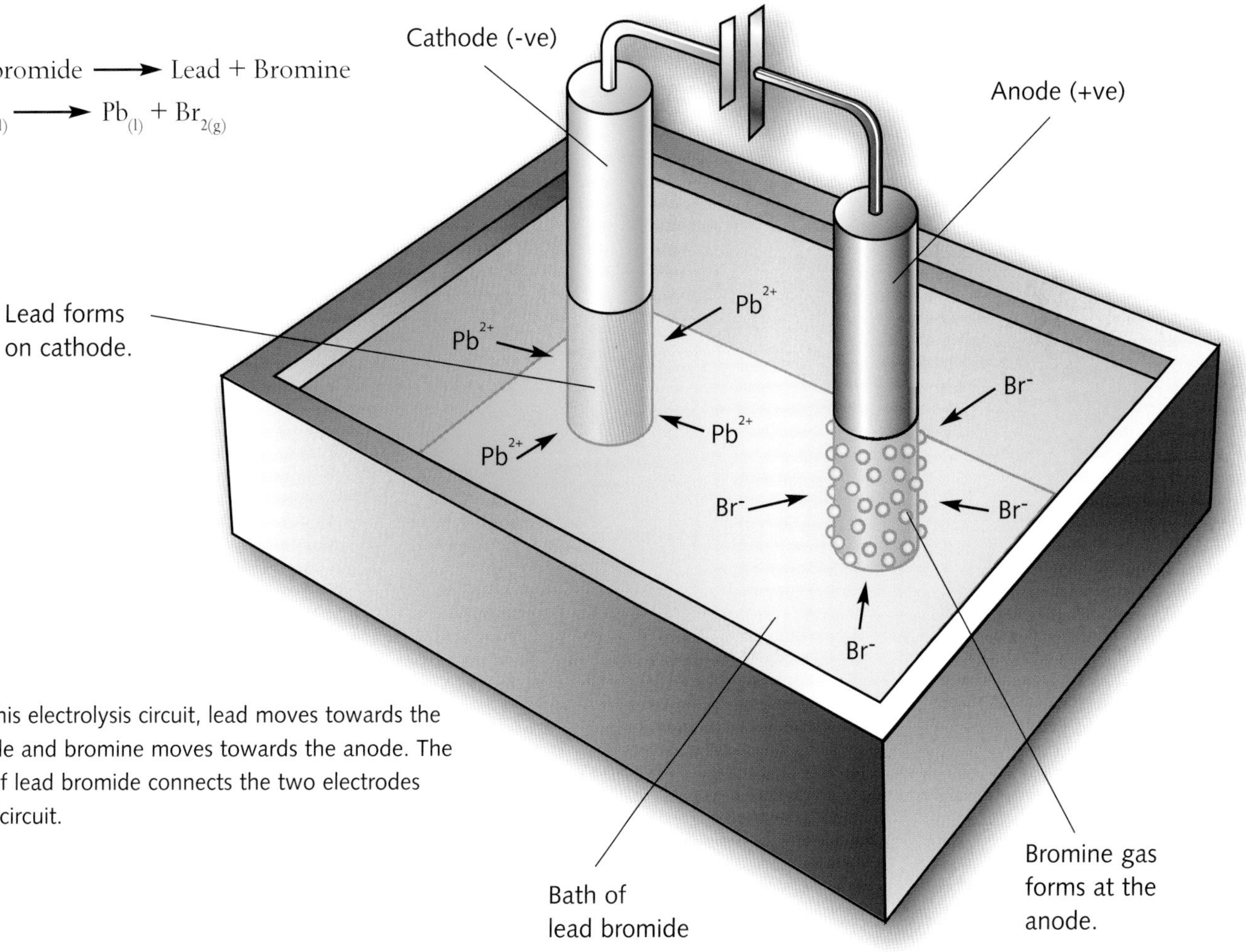

Cathode (-ve)

Anode (+ve)

Lead forms on cathode.

Pb^{2+}

Pb^{2+}

Pb^{2+}

Pb^{2+}

Br^-

Br^-

Br^-

Br^-

▶ In this electrolysis circuit, lead moves towards the cathode and bromine moves towards the anode. The bath of lead bromide connects the two electrodes in the circuit.

Bath of lead bromide

Bromine gas forms at the anode.

ELECTROLYSIS OF WATER

Water can be separated into hydrogen and oxygen by electrolysis. Pure water contains some positive hydrogen ions (H^+) and negative hydroxide ions (OH^-). Water is a weak conductor of electricity. When the electricity is switched on, negative hydroxide ions are attracted to the anode. Here they lose their extra electrons and form oxygen gas. The lost electrons are transferred to the cathode where they react with the positive hydrogen ions. Hydrogen gas is formed. The overall equation is:

Water $\longrightarrow$ Hydrogen + Oxygen

$$2H_2O_{(l)} \longrightarrow 2H_{2(g)} + O_{2(g)}$$

ELECTROLYSIS OF SOLUTIONS

When sodium chloride is dissolved in water, the Na^+ and Cl^- ions mix with the hydrogen ions (H^+) and hydroxide ions (OH^-) from the water.

WHAT HAPPENS AT THE CATHODE?

The H^+ ions and the Na^+ ions are attracted to the cathode. Hydrogen readily receives electrons that have come from the anode. It receives them more readily than other positive ions. First of all the hydrogen ion becomes a hydrogen atom, and then two atoms quickly join to form a hydrogen molecule. Sodium is not produced because hydrogen is better at accepting the electrons.

TIME TRAVEL: INTO THE FUTURE

Oil will run out in your lifetime. Scientists are searching for new ways to power cars. Fuel cells are one possibility and were first used in the 1960s in the Gemini-Apollo space programmes to generate electrical power and to produce drinking water. They convert hydrogen and oxygen into water. In doing so, electricity is produced which can be used to power other devices. Fuel cells are of particular interest to chemists who are concerned with environmental issues because:

▶ They have no moving parts, which means that they do not use up lots of energy.

▶ They do not emit any gases that can harm the Earth's atmosphere. The only waste product is water. The reaction that occurs in a hydrogen fuel cell is:

Hydrogen + Oxygen $\longrightarrow$ Water

$$2H_{2(g)} + O_{2(g)} \longrightarrow 2H_2O_{(g)}$$

◀ This hydrogen fuel cell bus is being trialled in Stuttgart in Germany.

What happens at the anode?

Cl^- and OH^- ions are attracted to the anode, but only chlorine gas is given off. This is because chloride ions are better at giving up their electrons than hydroxide ions. Therefore, the products formed during the electrolysis of aqueous solutions depends on the ability of the ions to be reduced or oxidised.

USES FOR ELECTROLYSIS

In a process called anodising, a piece of metal, such as aluminium, is made into the anode. The electrolyte contains a dye material. When the electricity is switched on, the aluminium anode takes up the colour of the dye. This gives us coloured metals, which are commonly used in bicycle frames, for example. Anodising is better than painting because the dye does not come off.

The same principle is used for covering one metal with another; this is called electroplating. Electroplating is used to cover steel parts of car bumpers and to silver-plate cutlery.

ELECTROPLATING

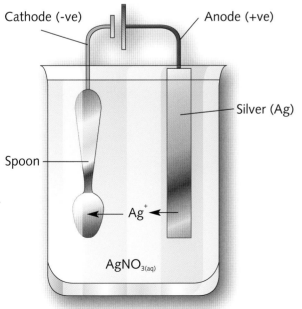

▲ A strip of silver is being used to silver-plate a spoon.

▼ Bicycle frames are anodised to give them colour.

TEST YOURSELF

▶ Which elements are gained from the electrolysis of the following molten compounds?
(1) Sodium chloride
(2) Copper iodide

Analysing chemical reactions

Chemists often analyse chemicals to determine their components. For example, forensic scientists analyse unknown substances found at crime scenes to determine what they are and whether they are related to the crime or the criminal. Chemists test the products of a chemical reaction in order to work out what reaction has taken place. The analysis of chemicals is methodical and involves many different tests.

TESTING FOR METAL IONS

If a chemist suspects that a substance contains metal ions (cations) there are two types of test to carry out.

(1) A flame test
(2) A precipitation test

(1) FLAME TEST

When some metals are placed into a blue flame, they produce distinctive colours. The chemist observes the colour and identifies the metal ion involved.

HOW TO CARRY OUT A FLAME TEST:

(a) Dip a nichrome wire into concentrated hydrochloric acid and place into a blue flame. Nichrome is a mixture of the metals nickel and chromium and it will not change colour when placed into a blue flame.

(b) If you can see a colour, repeat the first step until no colour appears. The wire is now clean.

(c) Next, dip the nichrome wire into concentrated hydrochloric acid and then into the sample to be tested. The sample should stick to the damp wire.

(d) Hold the sample in the flame and observe the colour change.

▲ A positive lithium flame test

Characteristic colours are produced for some metal ions, as shown in the following table:

Metal ion	Formula of ion	Colour
Lithium	Li^+	Scarlet red
Sodium	Na^+	Yellow
Potassium	K^+	Lilac
Barium	Ba^{2+}	Apple green
Copper	Cu^{2+}	Green
Calcium	Ca^{2+}	Brick red

(2) PRECIPITATION TEST

When two solutions are mixed together and an insoluble solid forms, precipitation has occurred. Certain metal ions produce certain coloured precipitates.

HOW TO CARRY OUT A PRECIPITATION TEST:

(a) Mix the test substance with sodium hydroxide solution.

(b) Observe the colour of the precipitate. Characteristic colours are produced for some metal ions, as shown in the following table:

Metal ion	Formula of ion	Colour of precipitate with sodium hydroxide
Iron (II)	Fe^{2+}	Green
Iron (III)	Fe^{3+}	Rusty brown
Copper (II)	Cu^{2+}	Blue
Nickel (II)	Ni^{2+}	Green
Cobalt (II)	Co^{2+}	Pink

◀ A positive precipitation test for copper.

Notice how a metal can form more than one type of metal ion. Iron can form two types of ion depending on how many electrons it has lost. Iron (II) has lost two electrons, whereas iron (III) has lost three electrons.

TESTING FOR AMMONIUM IONS

Ammonium ions have the formula NH_4^+. They are **complex ions** because they are made up from more than one type of element; in this case nitrogen and hydrogen. Ammonium ions are not metallic and will not give a positive test with a flame or precipitation test. They have a test all of their own. When chemists suspect that a solution contains ammonium ions, it is warmed and the gas that is emitted is tested with damp red litmus paper. The paper will turn blue as ammonia gas is given off. Ammonia gas also has a distinctive pungent smell.

TESTING FOR NON-METAL IONS

In the same way that chemists wish to find out which metal ions are in a mystery substance, they may also wish to find out about the non-metallic parts. These anions have their own chemical tests (see the following information on pages 34 and 35).

TEST YOURSELF

▶ A forensic chemist was asked to identify three solutions using precipitation tests. They knew that one of the solutions contained copper (II) ions, another iron (II) and the last iron (III) ions. What would the chemist do to identify the solutions and what results would they observe?

TESTING FOR HALIDES

Halides are non-metal ions from a group of the Periodic Table (see page 16) called the halogens. They include chloride (Cl^-), bromide (Br^-) and iodide (I^-) ions. Silver nitrate is used to test for halide ions. Firstly, dilute nitric acid is added to the test substance to remove any impurities. Next, silver nitrate solution is added and in the presence of a halide ion, a distinctive colour precipitate forms.

Anion	Formula of anion	Colour of precipitate	Name of precipitate	Formula of precipitate
Chloride	Cl^-	White	Silver chloride	AgCl
Bromide	Br^-	Cream	Silver bromide	AgBr
Iodide	I^-	Pale yellow	Silver iodide	AgI

The reactions that occur are:

Silver nitrate + Chloride → Silver chloride + Nitrate

Silver nitrate + Bromide → Silver bromide + Nitrate

Silver nitrate + Iodide → Silver iodide + Nitrate

Each of these three precipitates is sensitive to light. If they are left in bright sunshine, they turn grey.

TESTING FOR COMPLEX ANIONS

Complex anions contain more than one type of element. We can tell from their formula that they are complex because they have more than one capital letter. For example, a sulphate anion has the formula SO_4^{2-}. This tells us it has a negative charge, as we can see from the $2-$, and consists of the elements sulphur (S) and oxygen (O). Other complex anions include hydroxides (OH^-) and carbonates (CO_3^{2-}).

TESTING FOR SULPHATES

Chemists use a precipitation reaction to test for sulphates. Dilute nitric acid is added first,

▲ From left to right, these test tubes contain silver chloride, silver bromide and silver iodide.

followed by barium chloride solution. A white precipitate indicates the presence of a sulphate. This precipitate is not light-sensitive and is called barium sulphate. The reaction that has occurred is:

Barium chloride + Sodium sulphate → Barium sulphate + Sodium chloride

TESTING FOR CARBONATES

All carbonates react with acids to produce carbon dioxide gas.

Here is one example:

Calcium carbonate + Hydrochloric acid $\longrightarrow$ Calcium chloride + Water + Carbon dioxide

$$CaCO_{3(s)} + 2HCl_{(aq)} \longrightarrow CaCl_{2(aq)} + H_2O_{(l)} + CO_{2(g)}$$

When carbon dioxide is bubbled through calcium hydroxide solution, the solution turns milky.

▲ This forensic scientist is collecting evidence from a window. By chemically analysing trace (very small) chemicals she may be able to find out what smashed the window.

TEST YOURSELF

▶ Which elements and how many atoms of each element are present in the following complex anions?

Hydroxide (OH^-), Carbonate (CO_3^{2-})

▶ Flame tests were carried out on three unknown compounds, A, B and C. The results are given below.

Compound	Colour of flame
A	Lilac
B	Green
C	Yellow

Dilute nitric acid was then added to each compound. Next, a solution of silver nitrate was added. The results are given below.

Compound	Colour of precipitate
A	Yellow
B	White
C	Cream

What are A, B and C?

TIME TRAVEL: INTO THE FUTURE

In the future, chemical reactions may be used to build life from scratch. At the Los Alamos National Laboratory in the USA, a scientist called Steen Rasmussen has been awarded a US$5 million grant to carry out this research. He and his team hope to build a 'protocell', which will be a life form far smaller than a bacterium. This unique 'creature' will not resemble any life form that we currently know.

The ingredients for making the lifeform are a chemical called PNA, a chemical called pinacol and 'precursor molecules' that act as food for the protocell. In a mind-boggling series of chemical reactions, the scientists hope that the life form created will produce energy, grow and reproduce. If they succeed, they will be crossing the barrier between natural and human powers. Their work could provide new information about the origins of life on Earth.

10

Biological reactions

For thousands of years, humans have used organisms to create useful substances through chemical reactions. Yeast is a type of fungus. It contains chemicals called enzymes. Enzymes are biological catalysts. They speed up the conversion of reactants into products. In the case of yeast, the enzyme is called zymase. This aids the conversion of glucose into ethanol. Ethanol has many uses in fuels, drinks and as a solvent.

RESPIRATION

Respiration is the process that living organisms use to convert energy from their food into energy that they can use for living processes. When you mix together yeast and sugar, and keep the reactants in warm conditions, the following respiration reaction occurs:

$$\text{Glucose} \xrightarrow{\text{yeast}} \text{Ethanol} + \text{Carbon dioxide}$$

This process releases energy and proceeds without oxygen. We call this **anaerobic respiration**.

CONDITIONS FOR ETHANOL PRODUCTION

When the production of ethanol is carried out on an industrial scale, the reaction occurs in large containers called fermenters. The organisms inside the fermenters need each of the following conditions to ensure they carry out the reaction efficiently.

▶ **FOOD** – Yeast organisms need glucose as their food source. Different types of sugar produce different types of alcoholic drink. For example, wine is the fermentation product of grapes.

▼ This vat contains red wine. As the wine ferments it forms froth – bubbles of carbon dioxide.

▶ **Optimum temperature conditions** – Enzymes tend to function most efficiently at about 37°C. If the temperature is too high, the enzyme no longer functions. This process is called **denaturing**. If the temperature is too low, then fermentation will be very slow.

▶ **Limited amount of oxygen** – Yeast converts glucose to ethanol when there is a limited supply of oxygen. The air in the fermenter is mixed with extra carbon dioxide to limit the concentration of oxygen. The fermenter is sealed. Carbon dioxide produced during the reaction is allowed to escape through valves.

▶ **Mixing** – Industrial fermenters are fitted with stirrers. Constant mixing ensures as much of the sugar is converted into alcohol as possible. Not all of the sugar is converted to alcohol. This is because as the concentration of alcohol builds up, it destroys the yeast. The yeast becomes alcohol poisoned.

Uses of alcohol

Alcoholic drinks are prominent in many societies, but this is not the only use for alcohol. Ethanol is also an important solvent and is used in the manufacture of perfumes and aftershave. The scent is dissolved into ethanol and when this is sprayed onto the skin, the ethanol quickly evaporates and leaves the scent behind.

In Brazil, sugar cane is grown on a vast scale. It is fermented to produce ethanol which is mixed with petrol and used to fuel cars. The mixture is called gasohol.

Spoilage

Chemical reactions occur when bacteria come into contact with food. Bacteria feed on the food and spoil it. Eating food with bacteria on it can cause us ill health, such as sickness and diarrhoea. No bacteria are allowed access to the alcohol in a fermenter.

Time travel: Discoveries of the past

During the late 1700s and early 1800s, Napoleon's armies (right) were widely spread between Russia and Spain. They suffered from a lack of fresh food because their supply line was long and vulnerable. In 1795, Napoleon offered a prize of 12,000 Francs to anyone who could solve the food problem. This was awarded to Nicolas Appert, a French confectioner, in 1812. Appert came up with a method of sterilisation. He cooked food and placed it into an air-tight glass jar while it was still hot. This was the birth of the modern tin can, in which food can last up to 100 years.

How to speed up a reaction

Chemical reactions can happen instantly, or they can occur over many years or decades. For example, when sodium reacts with water, the explosion is almost instantaneous. On the other hand, copper roofing materials gradually oxidise and turn green over many years. Often, chemists need to speed up chemical reactions, particularly when they need to manufacture large quantities of chemicals in relatively short periods of time.

REACTION RATES

The rate of a chemical reaction is a measure of the amount of reactant that turns into product in a unit of time. The rate is important to a manufacturer because they need to meet demand for their product and must ensure they make a reasonable profit. The rate of a chemical reaction is not written as part of a balanced chemical equation. The only way to find out the speed is to carry out the experiment.

It is also important to realise that the reaction rate changes throughout one reaction. At the beginning of a reaction, a lot of reactant is present. As the reaction proceeds, some reactant is converted into product. The product does not react further and the reaction rate slows down. Eventually, when all the reactant has been converted into product, the reaction is complete. This can be displayed graphically.

RATE OF REACTION

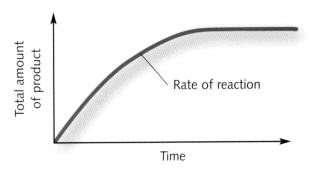

TEMPERATURE AND REACTION RATES

Temperature has a big effect on reaction rates. We use Bunsen burners to heat chemicals in the laboratory to make a reaction happen more quickly. In our homes, we place food in the fridge to slow down the reactions that spoil it. In fact, scientists have discovered that if the temperatures of some reactions are increased by 10°C, the rate of the reaction approximately doubles.

▲ Increasing the temperature of a reaction usually increases the reaction rate.

COLLISION THEORY – TEMPERATURE

During a chemical reaction, the reacting particles must collide with each other in order for the reaction to occur. However, when they do this, they must meet the following conditions:

▶ Reactants must collide with energy that is sufficient to break the chemical bonds.

▶ Reactants must collide at an angle that makes sure that all of their energy is put into the whole reaction.

AN UNSUCCESSFUL COLLISION

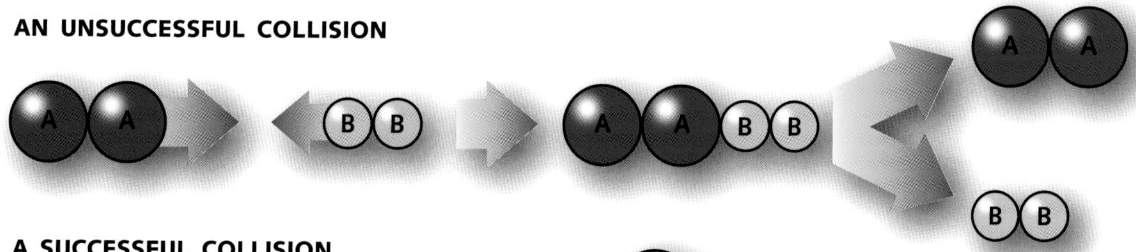

A SUCCESSFUL COLLISION

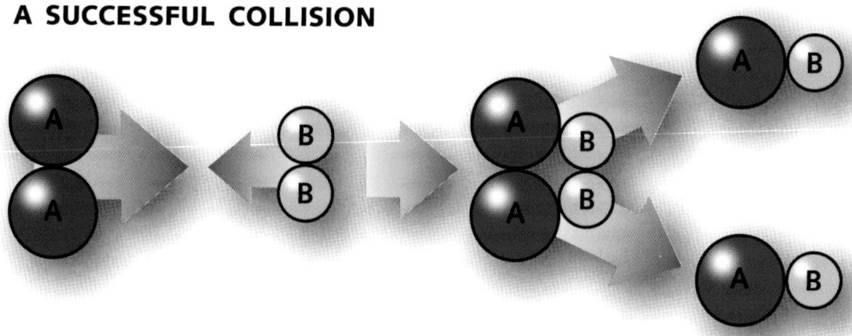

▲ The direction and angle with which the reactants collide affects the outcome.

As the temperature of a reaction increases, the following happens:

(1) The reacting particles gain more energy and move faster.
(2) The reacting particles collide with each other more frequently.
(3) The reacting particles have more energy and so the collisions are more likely to lead to a reaction.

RATE OF REACTION

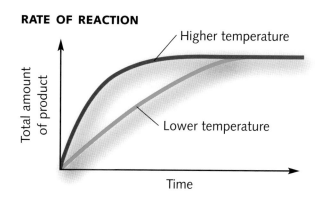

Higher temperature

Lower temperature

Total amount of product

Time

CONCENTRATION AND REACTION RATES

When you make a cup of hot chocolate, the instructions on the container tell you how many spoonfuls of chocolate powder to add. If you want a drink that is richer, it may be tempting to add more chocolate powder. This would give you a more concentrated drink.

The concentration of a solution is the amount of particles that have been dissolved into a given volume of water or other solvent. A high concentration has a lot of particles dissolved into it, whereas a low concentration has fewer. If concentrations of chemical solutions in a reaction are increased, the rate of reaction also increases. However, the final amount of end product does not increase.

▲ This magnesium ribbon is reacting with hydrochloric acid. The more concentrated the acid, the faster the reaction will proceed.

REACTING MAGNESIUM WITH HYDROCHLORIC ACID

The chemical equation for this reaction is:

Magnesium + Hydrochloric acid $\longrightarrow$ Magnesium chloride + Hydrogen

$$Mg_{(s)} + 2HCl_{(aq)} \longrightarrow MgCl_{2(aq)} + H_{2(g)}$$

It is possible to make this reaction proceed faster by increasing the concentration of the hydrochloric acid, whilst leaving all of the other conditions the same.

A chemist carried out this reaction with two samples of hydrochloric acid. Sample one was twice as concentrated as sample two. The chemist collected the hydrogen gas that was produced during each reaction. The graph below shows the results for these reactions. If we compare the two lines on the graph, the following becomes obvious:

(1) Sample one produces a line that is instantly steeper than sample two's line. This means that sample one produced more hydrogen gas than sample two in the same amount of time.

(2) Both lines eventually stop at the same volume of gas, because the *quantity* of reactant was the same in each reaction. Sample two reacted more slowly because it had fewer reacting particles for the same volume.

REACTING MAGNESIUM WITH HYDROCHLORIC ACID

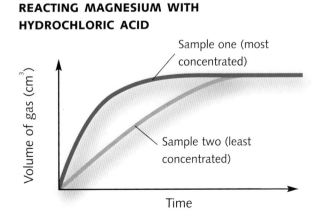

Sample one (most concentrated)

Sample two (least concentrated)

Volume of gas (cm^3)

Time

COLLISION THEORY – CONCENTRATION

This theory states that reactants are only converted to products if the reacting particles collide with each other with the required amount of energy and with a good orientation (see page 39). If the concentration of a solution is increased, the reaction is faster as there are more reacting particles in a given volume. This means there will be more collisions in a given period of time and therefore more collisions are likely to be successful and lead to products.

CONCENTRATION AND GASES

The same principle applies to gases under pressure. If a gas is compressed, the same number of gas particles are in a smaller space. The concentration has effectively increased. Reaction rates between gases are therefore increased by carrying out the reactions at higher pressures.

COMPRESSED GAS

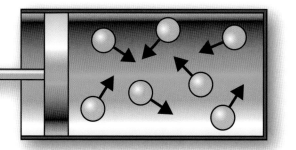

▲ Compare the two syringes. The gas in the syringe on the right has been compressed. The particles have been squeezed into a smaller place. This has increased the concentration.

CATALYSTS AND REACTION RATES

A catalyst increases the reaction rate. Because a catalyst is not chemically changed by the process, it can be used over and over again. For example, hydrogen peroxide decomposes very slowly at room temperature. The chemical equation is:

Hydrogen peroxide $\longrightarrow$ Water + Oxygen

$$2H_2O_{2(aq)} \longrightarrow 2H_2O_{(l)} + O_{2(g)}$$

If a bottle of hydrogen peroxide is left open for several years, all that would be left is water – if it has not all evaporated. This reaction can be speeded up by adding a catalyst called manganese (IV) oxide.

Manganese (IV) oxide is a transition metal. Compounds that contain transition metals make excellent catalysts. In the reaction with hydrogen peroxide, the manganese (IV) oxide immediately makes the hydrogen peroxide froth up as oxygen gas is produced. At the end of the reaction, the manganese (IV) oxide remains chemically unchanged and can be seen as a fine black powder in the reacting container.

CATALYST IN A REACTION

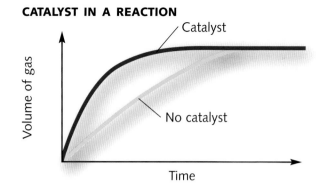

▲ This graph shows the effect of adding a catalyst to hydrogen peroxide. The catalyst speeds up the reaction.

HOW DO CATALYSTS WORK?

Catalysts provide a different route by which a reaction can occur. This is like a person who needs to get to the other side of a mountain. They can either spend a lot of energy going over the top of the mountain, or they can spend less energy by going through a tunnel bored through the middle. The overall result is the same, but the activation energy spent is much lower one way than the other. When catalysts are added to reactions, more reactants have the necessary energy and the reactions are much faster.

▶ Hydrogen peroxide in the beaker is decomposing. Manganese (IV) oxide is the catalyst. It speeds up the reaction.

DIFFERENT TYPES OF CATALYST

▶ Catalysts can exist in any physical state. If they are in the same physical state as the reactants, they are called **homogeneous**. Enzymes speed up the many reactions in our bodies. They work in an aqueous solution along with the reactants upon which they act.

▶ Catalysts that are in a different physical state to the reactants are called **heterogeneous**. The reaction involving manganese (IV) oxide and hydrogen peroxide is heterogeneous. Manganese (IV) oxide is a solid and hydrogen peroxide is in solution.

CATALYTIC CONVERTERS

All new cars are fitted with catalytic converters. They convert harmful exhaust fumes into less harmful products. Catalytic converters are made from the expensive metals platinum and rhodium. This is why it is expensive to buy a catalytic converter. Cheaper metals are not used because they are easily poisoned by the exhaust fumes.

Despite the fact that platinum and rhodium are expensive, it is still economically viable for them to be used, because if treated properly, they will never need to be replaced and they will never get used up. In addition, both metals can be extracted from the catalytic converters of scrapped cars and recycled.

WHAT HAPPENS IN A CATALYTIC CONVERTER?

(1) Carbon monoxide is converted into carbon dioxide.

(2) Partially burnt petrol is converted into carbon dioxide and water.

(3) Nitrogen oxides are converted into harmless nitrogen and oxygen.

(4) These safer gases are then emitted from the exhaust pipe.

▲ These cars are on their way to be recycled. Platinum and rhodium are retrieved from scrap cars and made into new catalytic converters.

TEST YOURSELF

▶ Hydrogen peroxide can also be broken down by a biological enzyme called catalase. Design an experiment to test which is better at breaking down hydrogen peroxide – catalase or manganese (IV) oxide.

SURFACE AREA AND REACTION RATES

In chemical reactions, larger pieces of reactant react more slowly than smaller pieces. When a solid is involved in a chemical reaction, the reaction takes place on the surface of the solid. The more surface that is exposed, the greater the rate of reaction.

Study the cube on this page. When the cube is cut in half, the exposed surface area increases, but the total volume remains the same. Therefore, when the cube is cut in half, there is a higher surface area to volume ratio than if there is just one large cube. The higher the surface area to volume ratio, the faster the rate of reaction.

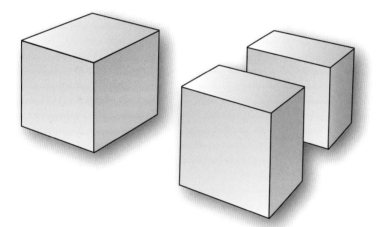

▲ The more pieces that a solid lump is cut into, the greater the surface area to volume ratio.

COLLISION THEORY – SURFACE AREA

The more successful collisions take place, the faster the reaction rate. Collisions take place on the surface of a solid. Therefore, a higher surface area to volume ratio will result in a faster reaction rate.

LIMESTONE AND ACID

The following chemical equation shows the reaction between calcium carbonate (limestone) and hydrochloric acid:

Calcium carbonate + Hydrochloric acid $\longrightarrow$ Calcium chloride + Water + Carbon dioxide

$$CaCO_{3(s)} + 2HCl_{(aq)} \longrightarrow CaCl_{2(aq)} + H_2O_{(l)} + CO_{2(g)}$$

The graph below shows what happens when different sized pieces of limestone, all of which have the same mass, react with the same concentration of hydrochloric acid.

REACTION RATE AND SURFACE AREA OF REACTANTS

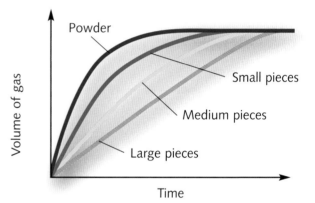

▲ The smaller the particle size, the greater the surface area to volume ratio and the more rapidly the reaction proceeds. The amount of final product remains the same.

▲ Both beakers contain hydrochloric acid and calcium carbonate – as a powder on the left and as a single piece on the right. The reaction rate is faster when the surface area is greater.

The reaction occurs on the surface of the limestone pieces. When the limestone is in powder form, the maximum surface area is exposed and the reaction is almost instantaneous. Lots of gas is given off very quickly. If large pieces of limestone are used, a much smaller area is available for reaction at any one time. As the outer layer of limestone reacts, a fresh part is exposed and now available for reaction. The reaction appears to be more gradual and it may look as though not much is happening. As all of these experiments involve the same mass of limestone, the final amount of gas given off is exactly the same.

MEASURING MASS TO FIND OUT REACTION RATE

The reaction of limestone and hydrochloric acid can also be followed by measuring the loss in mass. Gas produced by the reaction can escape the flask through a loose plug of cotton wool. The acid may spray, so the cotton wool is necessary for safety and to prevent a false loss in mass. As the carbon dioxide escapes, the contents of the flask become lighter. If mass is recorded at regular time periods, you will find that there is a gradual loss in mass. When plotted on a graph, this is a measure of reaction rate.

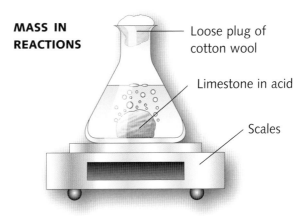

MASS IN REACTIONS

Loose plug of cotton wool

Limestone in acid

Scales

▲ The mass will decrease as the reaction between the limestone and the acid proceeds.

▲ You can see the bubbles of carbon dioxide coming from the outside layer of this piece of limestone.

INVESTIGATE

▶ **Ask an adult's permission before you carry out this investigation.**
Investigate the effect of an increased surface area to volume ratio by making some cheese on toast. Weigh slices of cheese and then place them on one slice of bread. Grate the same mass of cheese onto another slice of bread. Place both slices under the grill. Which slice of bread and cheese cooks first? Why?

Glossary

ANAEROBIC RESPIRATION – Respiration in the absence of oxygen.

ANION – A negatively-charged atom.

ANODE – A positive electrode.

BOIL – To heat a liquid to its boiling point. At this temperature it will undergo a physical change from a liquid to a gas.

CATALYST – A substance used to speed up a chemical reaction without itself being used up or changed.

CATHODE – A negative electrode.

CATION – A positively-charged atom.

CHEMICAL BONDS – The forces that hold two or more atoms together in a substance.

COMBUSTION – The reaction between a fuel and oxygen that produces heat and/or light. It is also called burning.

COMPLEX ION – An ion made up from more than one type of atom.

CONDENSE – A physical change from a gas to a liquid.

CORRODE – The chemical breakdown of a substance. The rusting of iron is a type of corrosion.

DELOCALISED – A delocalised electron is free to move, rather than being bound to a particular atom.

DENATURE – To permanently alter the shape of a protein, such as an enzyme.

DIFFUSION – The movement of a substance from an area where it is plentiful to an area where it is less plentiful.

DISPLACEMENT – When one substance is removed from a compound by another more reactive substance.

ELECTROLYSIS – This process involves passing electricity through a compound to split it into its elements.

ANSWERS

p9 Investigate
(1) Stage smoke = a physical change.
(2) Hydrogen and oxygen changing into water = a chemical change.
(3) Hand warmers = a chemical change or a physical change. There are many types of hand warmer. Some involve the rapid oxidation of iron when it is exposed to air. This chemical change gives out heat. Some contain two different chemicals, which when shaken together result in a chemical change that produces heat. Other hand warmers contain sodium acetate solution. When a disc in the sodium acetate solution is bent, it causes the sodium acetate to crystallise and become a solid – a physical change.

p11 Test yourself
(1) Light.
(2) Exposure to water.

p15 Test yourself
(1)
$$Carbon + Oxygen \xrightarrow{heat} Carbon\ dioxide$$
(2)
$$Magnesium + Oxygen \xrightarrow{heat} Magnesium\ oxide$$
(3)
$$Methane + Chlorine \xrightarrow{u.v.} Chloromethane + Hydrogen\ chloride$$
(4)
$$Hydrogen\ peroxide \xrightarrow{catalase} Water + Oxygen$$

p18 Test yourself
(1) Copper oxide CuO, (2) Iron chloride $FeCl_2$ or $FeCl_3$, (3) Aluminium bromide $AlBr_3$, (4) Calcium oxide CaO

p19 Test yourself
(1) $2H_{2(g)} + O_{2(g)} \longrightarrow 2H_2O_{(l)}$
(2) $2Na_{(s)} + Cl_{2(g)} \longrightarrow 2NaCl_{(s)}$

(3) $2Mg_{(s)} + O_{2(g)} \longrightarrow 2MgO_{(s)}$

p21 Test yourself
The chemist must use fresh samples from each bottle for each test. Firstly, the chemist should add sodium hydroxide to a sample of each chemical. He/she can identify the metal in the compound by comparing the colour of the precipitate to the table on page 21. Next, he/she should add a small volume of dilute nitric acid to a new sample of each chemical to removes impurities. Next, he/she should add silver nitrate and compare the colours to the photograph on page 34.

p21 Investigate
When a firework is ignited, oxygen gas is produced by the thermal decomposition of potassium nitrate. The pressure builds up inside the firework casing and causes it to shoot into the

ENDOTHERMIC – Reactions in which overall heat energy is taken in from the surroundings. Endothermic reactions feel cold.

ENZYME – A biological catalyst.

EVAPORATION – A physical change from a liquid to a gas.

EXOTHERMIC – Reactions in which overall heat energy is given out.

FREEZE – A physical change from a liquid to a solid.

HETEROGENEOUS – Two substances in different physical states.

HOMOGENEOUS – Two substances in the same physical state.

IMMISCIBLE – Substances that will not mix.

MELT – A physical change from a solid to a liquid.

MISCIBLE – Substances that will mix together.

OXIDISER – A chemical that contains a lot of oxygen and can oxidise another chemical.

PARTICULATES – Fine particles in air or water.

PRECIPITATE – An insoluble solid formed when two solutions react together.

PRODUCTS – Chemicals resulting from a chemical reaction.

REACTANTS – Starting materials for a chemical reaction.

REDOX – Reduction and oxidation reactions occurring together.

SUSPENSION – A fine solid distributed in a liquid.

Useful websites:
http://www.chem4kids.com
http://www.howstuffworks.com
http://www.bbc.co.uk/schools
http://www.sciencenewsforkids.org
http://www.newscientist.com

---

air. The oxygen also helps the fuel to burn.

p23 Test yourself
Combustion takes place in central heating systems, in a car's engine, when a match is lit, and in coal-burning power stations, which produce electricity.

p25 Test yourself
(1) CuO is reduced because it has lost oxygen; H_2 is oxidised because it has gained oxygen.
(2) Mg has been oxidised because it has gained oxygen; O must therefore be reduced.
(3) Mg is oxidised because it has gained oxygen; SO_2 has lost oxygen, therefore is reduced.

p25 Investigate
Halogens at the top of the group are more reactive than those at the bottom. The more reactive halogens can displace less reactive halogens from their compounds.

p31 Test yourself
(1) Sodium and chlorine, (2) Copper and iodine

p33 Test yourself
Add sodium hydroxide solution. Copper (II) gives a blue precipitate, Iron (II) a green precipitate and Iron (III) a rust coloured precipitate.

p35 Test yourself
Hydroxide = one oxygen and one hydrogen atom.
Carbonate = one carbon and three oxygen atoms.
A is potassium iodide, B is copper chloride and C is sodium bromide.

p39 Test yourself
The graph will be a progress curve with a shape similar to that on page 38. At 10°C the line will be shallower and will not go any higher than about 10 cm³. At 40°C the line will rise more sharply, but will go no higher than 17 cm³.

Particles that react with milk and spoil it have less energy at lower temperatures. There are fewer collisions and the reaction is much slower.

p41 Test yourself
(1) Increase the number of pupils. (2) Partition off some of the playground so that the pupils are in a smaller space.

p43 Test yourself
Use the same amount of hydrogen peroxide for testing both catalysts. Use the same mass of each catalyst. Record the amount of froth produced in a given unit of time for each catalyst. The one that produces the most froth is better at breaking down hydrogen peroxide.

p45 Investigate
The slice of bread with grated cheese cooks first. It has a greater surface area to volume ratio.

Index

Page references in italics
represent pictures.

acid 13, 32, 35, 40, *40*, 44
air 23
alcohol 36, 37
ammonia 26, 27, 33
ammonium 33
anaerobic respiration 36, 46
anaesthetics 21
anhydrous compounds 20, *20*, 26
anions 29, 33, 34, 46
anode 29, 30, 31, 46
anodising 30
atoms 6, 10, 11, 12, 16, 17, 18, 19, 22,
    24, 25, 28, 29, 30, 46, 47

bacteria 37
biological reactions 36, 37
bleaching 25, *25*,
boiling 6, 46

carbonates 35, *35*, 40, 47
cars 9, 23, *23*, 30, 41, 43, 47
catalyst 15, *15*, 27, 36, 42, *42*, 43,
    46, 47
catalytic converters 43, *43*
cathode 29, 30, 31, 46
cations 29, 46
chemical bonds 7, 10, 11, 12, 13, 14,
    22, 24, 39, 46
chemical change 6, 7, 14, 15, 16, 18,
    22, 26, 46
chemical symbols 16, 18, 27
collision theory 39, *39*, 41, 44, 47
colour change 12
combustion 8, *8*, 12, 18, 20, 22, *22*,
    23, 46
complex ions 33, 34, 35, 46
compounds 11, 14, 16, 17, 18, 20, 21,
    24, 25, 28, 47
concentration 40, 41, *41*
condensation 6, 46
corroded 7, 46

Davy lamp 9
Davy, Sir Humphry 21, *21*
decomposition 15, 20
delocalised 28, 46
denaturing 36, 46
diffusion 23, 46
displacement 24, 25, 46

electricity 23, 28, 29, 30, 31, 47
electrochemical cell 29

electrolysis 28, 29, *29*, 30, 31, 47
electrons 17, 24, 25, 28, 30, 31, 33,
    42, 46
electroplating 30, *30*
elements 11, 14, 16, 23, 24, 25, 28,
    33, 34, 35, 47
endothermic reactions 12, 13, 46
energy 6, 8, 10, 11, 12, 13, 22, 31, 35,
    36, 39, 41, 42, 46, 47
engines 8, 41
enzyme 15, *15*, 27, 36, 43, 46, 47
equations 14, 15, 16, 18, 19, 26, 27,
    30, 38
    balancing 18, 19, 38
equilibrium 26
ethanol (see alcohol)
evaporation 20, 42, 47
exothermic reactions 12, 13, *13*, 22, 47
explosions 8, 9, 10, 12, 26, 38

fermentation 36, 37
fire triangle 22, *22*, 23
fireworks 8, 21, 46
flame tests 32, *32*
formulae 14, 16, 17, 18, 19
freezing 6, 47
fuel 9, 22, 23, 37, 41, 46
fuel cells 31

gas 41, *41*, 43, 45, 46, 47
gunpowder 8, 9

Haber Process 27, *27*
halides 34
halogens 25, 34, 47
heat 10, 11, 12, 13, 14, 20, 22
heterogeneous 43, 47
homogeneous 43, 47
hydrated compounds 20, *20*, 26, *26*
hydration 26, *26*

immiscible 7, *7*, 47
ions 11, 17, 28, *28*, 29, 30, 31, 32,
    33, 34, 46, 47

light 10, 11, 15, 20, 22
lime 20
limestone 20, *20*, 44, 45

matches 11, *11*
melting 6, 28, 47
metals 10, 21, 23, 28, 30, 32, 33, 43
methane 12, *12*, 13
mining 8, 9, 24, *24*
miscible 7, 47

molecules 6, 7, 10, 11, 19, 47
motion 10

Napoleon 37, *37*
neutralisation 20
non-metals 33, 34

oil 31
oxidation 24, 25, 31, 38, 46, 47

particulates 23, 47
periodic table 16, *16*, 34
photosynthesis 10
physical change 6, 7, 46, 47
precipitates 21, *21*, 33, *33*, 34, *34*,
    46, 47
precipitation 20, 21, 33, *33*
    test 32, 33, *33*, 34, *34*
Priestley, Joseph 21
products 7, 9, 11, 12, 14, 15, 16, 18,
    19, 20, 21, 22, 24, 26, 27, 32, 36, 38,
    41, 47

reactants 7, 10, 11, 12, 14, 15, 16, 18,
    19, 26, 27, 36, 38, 39, 41, 43, 44, 47
reaction rates 38, *38*, 39, *39*, 40, 41, 42,
    43, 44, 45, *45*, 47
redox 24, 47
reduction 24, 25, 31, 47
respiration 36, 46
reversible reactions 26, 27
rockets 8, 9, *9*
rusting 7, 10

salts 7, 28
sodium chloride 7, 28, *28*, 31
solar power 31
spoilage 37, 38, 47
starting a reaction 10
states of matter 6, *6*, 7
state symbols 19
sterilisation 37
sulphates 34
surface area 43, 44, *44*, 45
suspension 21, *21*, 47
swap and drop 16, 17, 18

thermal decomposition 20, 21
transition metals 42

Walker, John 11
water 10, 20, 30, 31
weathering 6

yeast 36, *36*, 37

PHOTO CREDITS – *(abbv: r, right, l, left, t, top, m, middle, b, bottom)* **Cover background image** www.istockphoto.com/Jon Helgason **Front cover images** (r) www.istockphoto.com/jallfree (l) www.istockphoto.com/foto pfluegl **Back cover image** (inset) www.istockphoto.com/jallfree **p.1** (t) David Taylor/Science Photo Library (br) NASA (bl) Tek Image/Science Photo Library **p.2** www.istockphoto.com/Justin Allfree **p.3** (b) www.istockphoto.com/Klaas Lingbeek-van Kranen (t) Erich Schrempp/Science Photo Library **p.4** (tr) www.istockphoto.com/Feng Yu (tl) Andrew Lambert Photography/Science Photo Library (br) Martin Bond/Science Photo Library **p.5** Charles D. Winters/Science Photo Library **p.7** Kip Peticolas/Fundamental Photo/Science Photo Library **p.8** Erich Schrempp/Science Photo Library **p.9** NASA **p.10** Andrew Lambert Photography/Science Photo Library **p.11** www.istockphoto.com/Ethan Gibbs **p.12** Robert Brook/Science Photo Library **p.14** (both) Martyn F. Chillmaid/Science Photo Library **p.15** Martyn F. Chillmaid/Science Photo Library **p.19** Charles D. Winters/Science Photo Library **p.20** (t) www.istockphoto.com/Jonathan Klemenz (m) Andrew Lambert Photography/Science Photo Library (b) Andrew Lambert Photography/Science Photo Library **p.21** (t) Sheila Terry/Science Photo Library (b) Andrew Lambert Photography/Science Photo Library **p.22** (b) Reuters/Corbis **p.23** www.istockphoto.com/Klaas Lingbeek-van Kranen **p.24** Jacques Jangoux/Science Photo Library **p.25** R. Maisonneuve, Publiphoto Diffusion/Science Photo Library **p.26** Andrew Lambert Photography/Science Photo Library **p.30** Martin Bond/Science Photo Library **p.31** (r) www.istockphoto.com/Justin Allfree **p.32** Andrew Lambert Photography/Science Photo Library **p.33** Andrew Lambert Photography/Science Photo Library **p.34** Andrew Lambert Photography/Science Photo Library **p.35** Tek Image/Science Photo Library **p.36** Charles O'Rear/Corbis **p.37** Corbis **p.38** Richard Megna/Fundamental Photos/Science Photo Library **p.40** Charles D. Winters/Science Photo Library **p.41** John Walsh/Science Photo Library **p.42** Charles D. Winters/Science Photo Library **p.43** www.istockphoto.com/Feng Yu **p.44** Martyn F. Chillmaid/Science Photo Library **p.45** David Taylor/Science Photo Library